Punjabi Style Recipes

A Complete Cookbook of Northern India Dish Ideas!

Table of Contents

Introduction

Have you discovered how popular Punjabi cuisine has become, in India and Pakistan and now in other countries worldwide?

If you've eaten Punjabi dishes, you may be intrigued to know that you can make many at home. Some ingredients are substituted, as noted in the recipes, but many translate very well.

The Punjab region offers exotic and delectable meat and vegetable dishes, prepared using the traditional Punjabi culinary style. Their finger-licking, mouth-watering dishes will find a place in your home, and your family will probably be asking for more samples of Punjabi cuisine, once they have had their first taste.

Punjabi meals are often made with butter or clarified butter. If you want to use healthier oils like canola or sunflower, you can substitute them. Some of their favorite spices include ginger, garlic, onion and fenugreek leaves. They also are fond of using condiments like black pepper, methi leaves, coriander and cumin.

Sugarcane is grown in Northern India, as are millet, potatoes and barley. They raise cattle for their milk, and to make paneer (cottage cheese) and clarified butter. Dairy is integral to their diet.

Want to try some of their recipes for yourself? Turn the page, let's cook Punjabi style.

Punjabi Breakfast Recipes...

1 – Fenugreek Corn Roti and Spinach

This is a healthy flat bread dish that uses maize flour as its main ingredient. It's a vegan dish, as well, since the ingredients are all natural. Palak, or spinach curry, is a healthy ingredient. This meal is often served during the weekday mornings.

Makes 5 Servings

Cooking + Prep Time: 40 minutes

Ingredients:

- 1 cup of flour, maize
- 3/4 cup of spinach, chopped
- 1/4 cup of fenugreek leaves, chopped
- 1 1/2 tsp. of chili paste, green
- Salt, sea, as desired
- 2 tsp. of sesame seeds
- 3 tsp. of oil, olive
- To roll - flour, all-purpose

Instructions:

1. Combine 1/2 tsp. oil, sesame seeds, salt, chili paste, fenugreek leaves, spinach and flour in large bowl. Knead, making a dough that is somewhat stiff. Add water if needed.

2. Divide dough in five equal portions. Use a bit of flour and roll them into 5-inch diameter circles.

3. Heat griddle. Cook roti's over med. heat. Use 1/2 tsp. oil till roti's have light brown spots on both sides. Serve promptly.

2 – Chana Kulcha

This tasty breakfast dish bursts forth with flavors from the start, with spicy chick peas. It's an especially popular recipe in the Punjab region. It goes great with kulcha flat breads.

Makes 2 Servings

Cooking + Prep Time: 40 minutes + six to seven hours overnight and boiling time

Ingredients:

- 2 tsp. of baking soda
- 2 1/4 lbs. of chickpeas
- For masala

- 2 tsp. of mango powder, if available
- 3 tsp. of salt, sea
- 2 tsp. of powdered black pepper
- 1 tsp. of chili powder, red
- 2 tsp. each of powdered clove and powdered cinnamon
- 2 tsp. each of cumin powder, carom powder and coriander powder
- 2 tsp. of ginger, dry

Instructions:

1. Soak the chickpeas overnight in baking soda and water.

2. Boil chickpeas in water over low heat for six to seven hours for the best taste.

3. Add cinnamon, carom, coriander, ginger, clove, cumin, powdered black pepper, red chili powder, mango powder and sea salt.

4. Mix well. Serve while hot.

3 – Lucky Paratha

This is among the more popular of flat breads in Northern India, and you'll know why as soon as you see it. It is layered and has an appealing and appetizing look. The parathas melt in your mouth, too, so they're a great choice for breakfast.

Makes 7 Servings

Cooking + Prep Time: 35 minutes

Ingredients:

- 2 tbsp. of butter, clarified
- 2 cups of flour, whole wheat
- Sea salt, as desired
- To roll and sprinkle: flour, whole wheat
- To brush: 7 tsp. of clarified butter
- To cook: 7 tsp. of clarified butter

Instructions:

1. Combine flour, sea salt and 2 tbsp. of clarified butter in deep, large bowl. Combine. Knead into soft dough with lukewarm water as needed.

2. Divide dough into seven portions of equal size.

3. Use a bit of flour and roll portions of dough into 8-inch diameter rounds.

4. Evenly spread 1 tsp. of clarified butter over dough.

5. Sprinkle a bit of flour over circles. Spread lightly.

6. Fold each circle from one end to other, making fan-like pleats. Press in the pleats as you make them.

7. Roll circles over again from one end to other. Form swiss rolls. Seal open ends tightly in middle and at bottom.

8. Turn swiss rolls over so sealed side is facing up. Roll gently again into 6-inch diameter circles. Use flour as needed to roll.

9. Heat griddle. Cook paratha with a tsp. of clarified butter, till you see light brown spots on both sides.

10. Remove paratha to plate. Press gently from sides toward middle, making the layers easier to see. Serve hot with chilled curds.

4 – Vegetable Samosas

This is one samosa recipe that's easy to make. Indian samosas have flaky crusts made from Indian flour, stuffed with spiced peas and potatoes. You'll never believe how little work it takes to create them.

Makes various number of servings

Cooking + Prep Time: 1 hour 15 minutes

Ingredients:

For the cover

For kneading: water

- 1 cup of flour, all-purpose

- A bit of salt, sea
- 2 tbsp. of oil, olive

For the stuffing

- 1/2 cup of boiled green peas
- 3 or 4 boiled, peeled, mashed potatoes
- 1 or 2 chopped chilies, green
- 1/2 tsp. of crushed ginger
- 1 tbsp. of chopped coriander
- Several cashews, chopped, as desired
- Several raisins, as desired
- 1/2 tsp. of Garam masala spice blend
- Salt, as desired
- Chili powder, red, as desired

Instructions:

1. To prepare the cover, mix all cover ingredients with the exception of the water.

2. Then add the water, a bit at a time.

3. Pat the dough and knead it well a few times till it's pliable and soft.

4. Cover with damp Muslin cloth. Set aside for 10-15 minutes.

5. To prepare the stuffing, add all the dry masalas and mashed potatoes, plus chilies and ginger. Mix and combine well.

6. Add raisins, green peas and cashews. Combine thoroughly.

7. Add coriander. Set aside.

8. To prepare the samosas, make rolls from dough. Roll them into 4-inch diameter circles. Slice them in semi circles, in two parts.

9. Fold a semi-circle into a cone. Use water to help you.

10. Place spoonful of filling in cone. Seal third side with water.

11. Heat oil in griddle. Deep fry on med. heat till each is golden brown. Serve hot, with chutney, if you like.

5 – Flattened Rice Breakfast - Poha

Poha is a healthy, delicious, easy breakfast dish, quite popular in the Punjab region. It's made with potatoes and onions, along with seasonings that include curry leaves, chilies and lemon. It's a great breakfast to make when you really don't want to cook all morning.

Makes 2 Servings

Cooking + Prep Time: 40 minutes

Ingredients:

- 1 cup of rice, pressed (poha)
- 1 tbsp. of oil, olive

- 1/8 tsp. of dried herb gum - asafoetida
- 1/2 cup of chopped onions
- 1 tsp. of mustard seeds
- 8 to 10 leaves of curry
- 2 to 3 red chilies, whole
- 1/2 cup of diced potatoes
- 1/2 tsp. of turmeric
- 2 tsp. of salt, sea
- 1 tsp. of chopped chilies, green
- 1 tbsp. of chopped coriander leaves
- 1 tbsp. of lemon juice, fresh

For garnishing: lemon wedges, fresh

Instructions:

1. Place rice in colander. Wash. Don't let it soak for too long. Drain and allow to set in colander for complete draining.

2. Heat oil. Add herb gum, red chilies, onions, curry leaves and mustard seeds.

3. When the onions have browned lightly, add the potatoes. Turn them around till they appear slightly glossy.

4. Add turmeric. Sauté on low heat till potatoes cook through completely.

5. Raise heat to medium. Add rice and sea salt. Combine well, then sauté till heated through and mixed.

6. Turn heat off. Add and mix 1/2 of coriander, plus green chilies and lemon juice.

7. Transfer to serving dish. Use lemon wedges and remainder of coriander for garnishing. Serve.

Punjabi Recipes for Lunches, Dinners, Side Dishes and Appetizers...

6 – Mushroom Achari

This is an interesting dish, to be sure. The mushrooms are soaking in the spice flavors and you can use nearly any type of mushroom you like, whether it's portabella, shiitake, cremini or button. It goes quite well with naan flat bread or roti.

Makes 10 Servings

Cooking + Prep Time: 40 minutes

Ingredients:

- 1 lb. of mushrooms
- 1/2 tsp. of nigella seeds
- 1 tsp. of fennel seeds
- 1 tbsp. of paste, ginger
- 1 tbsp. of powdered coriander seeds
- 1/2 tsp. of turmeric
- 1/2 tsp. of pepper, cayenne
- 2 tsp. of paste, garlic
- 2 diced tomatoes, large
- Sea salt, as desired
- 1 tsp. of oil, coconut
- 1/4 cup of cilantro, chopped

Instructions:

1. Heat coconut oil in large sized sauce pan.

2. Add fennel and nigella seeds. Toast for 2 minutes or so on med-low heat till they have released their aroma. It is very distinct – you won't miss it.

3. Add garlic and ginger. Stir-fry for 10 to 15 seconds. Next, add tomatoes and juice. Stir and combine.

4. Add cayenne pepper, turmeric and coriander powder. Combine thoroughly. Allow tomatoes to cook till they shimmer and darken.

5. Add mushrooms. Add sea salt, as desired. Combine well. Allow mushrooms to cook for five to seven more minutes till they're tender. Don't let them get soggy, though.

6. Remove from heat. Stir in cilantro. Serve hot.

7 – Punjabi Tawa Fish

This is another popular recipe in the North of India. You can prepare it for any occasion, or for no occasion at all. It is usually served as an appetizer and it's a favorite at potlucks and parties.

Makes 3 Servings

Cooking + Prep Time: 1 hour 5 minutes

Ingredients:

- 7 oz. of fish, rohu (Asian carp)
- 1/4 tsp. of turmeric
- 1 tsp. of coriander leaves
- 1/2 tsp. of chili powder, red
- 7 oz. of flour, rice
- 3 1/3 fluid oz. of oil, mustard
- 1 fluid oz. of lemon juice, fresh
- Sea salt, as desired
- 1 tsp. of coriander powder
- 1 egg, large
- 1 oz. of flour, besan
- 1/2 tsp. of chaat masala blend

For the marinating

- 1/2 tbsp. of paste, garlic
- 1/8 fluid oz. of vinegar, white
- 1/4 tsp. of powdered Garam masala spice blend

For main dish

- 1/2 tbsp. of paste, ginger

Instructions:

1. Wash fish well under cold water. Marinate with combined marinating ingredients above. Place in the refrigerator for 1/2 hour.

2. Add rice powder, flour, egg and other ingredients to large bowl. Combine to create your batter.

3. Place pan on med. heat. Add oil. Heat the oil and fry fish till crispy on both sides.

4. Sprinkle chaat masala on fish. Serve hot with lemon wedges and chutney, if desired.

8 – Dal Bukhara

This is one of the classic Punjabi curries, made from black urad dal. It's creamy and it melts in your mouth. It tastes especially good with roti or rice. Take your time allowing it to simmer long enough, since that's how you'll get its proper, creamy texture.

Makes 10 Servings

Cooking + Prep Time: 1 hour

Ingredients:

- 1 1/2 cups of skin-on udad dal
- 1 tsp. of oil, vegetable

- 2 tbsp. of coriander powder
- 2 tsp. of Garam masala spice blend
- 2 tsp. of powdered cumin
- 1 tsp. of pepper, cayenne
- 1 tsp. of cumin seeds
- 1/2 tsp. of turmeric
- 1 x 1" knob of grated ginger, fresh
- 1 tbsp. of paste, garlic
- 1 1/2 cups of pureed tomatoes
- 1/4 cup of fenugreek leaves, dry – available in Indian grocery stores
- Sea salt, as desired
- 1 tbsp. of butter, unsalted
- 1/2 cup of coriander, chopped

Instructions:

1. Heat oil and add cumin seeds. After they have darkened a bit, add garlic and ginger. Sauté for several seconds.

2. Add cumin and coriander powder, then turmeric and cayenne. Cook while stirring till tomato puree has darkened and most moisture has fully evaporated.

3. Cook dal till very tender. (Presoaking overnight is helpful.) Cook in pan on burner with an inch or more water to cover. It usually takes an hour or so till the dal become very soft.

4. Add cooked dal to original pan. Combine well. Add water if dal seems too thick. It should be somewhat thick, but still runny.

5. Bring dal to boil and lower heat. Allow it to simmer for 10 more minutes.

6. Add and stir in Garam masala spice blend. Add butter, then sea salt, as desired.

7. Sprinkle coriander into dal. Turn off heat. Serve hot with naan flatbread or rice.

9 – Bhatti da Murga Pindiwala

If you visit the Punjab region, you will see many street vendors selling this favorite food on the streets. It is cooked for street sale on charcoal grills. When you marinate the chicken overnight in high-quality spices, the taste is amazing.

Makes 4 Servings

Cooking + Prep Time: 55 minutes + 6-8 hours marinating time

Ingredients:

- 8 bone-in legs of chicken
- To baste: clarified butter

For marinating

- 3 tbsp. of oil, cooking
- 5 tsp. of strained garlic paste
- 3 1/2 tsp. of strained ginger paste
- 3 tbsp. of whisked yogurt
- 4 tbsp. of vinegar, malt
- 2 tsp. of pepper, black
- 2 tsp. of powdered pomegranate
- 1 1/2 tsp. powdered each of black cardamom, cinnamon, cumin and coriander
- 1 tsp. powdered each of nutmeg, green cardamom, clove, allspice, mace and nutmeg
- 1 pinch of powdered fenugreek leaf, dried
- 1 pinch salt, sea

Instructions:

1. To prepare chicken, clean well. Make deep, angular incisions – 2 on drumsticks and 3 on thighs.

2. To prepare marinade, heat the oil in wok. Add ginger and garlic. Stir-fry on med. heat till moisture has evaporated.

3. Remove from the heat. Add and stir yogurt. Combine well. Transfer mixture to large sized bowl. Allow to cool.

4. When mixture is cool, add remaining marinade ingredients and combine well.

5. Rub chicken legs using marinade. Set aside for six to eight hours.

6. Place marinated chicken in batches on grill. Roast on med. heat for five to six minutes. Turn once while roasting. Use clarified butter to baste at regular time periods.

7. Remove chicken. Separate thigh bones from drumstick bones. Don't separate meat.

8. Place chicken back on the grill. Roast for two or three minutes more. Turn and baste one time before you're done. Serve hot.

10 – Puri Bhaji

Here is another delicious meal from Northern India. It's one of the favorite dinners of people who live in the region, as well as visitors to the area. The crispy texture and astounding aroma will blow your taste buds away.

Makes 4 Servings

Cooking + Prep Time: 40 minutes

Ingredients:

- 4 potatoes, boiled, then peeled, then mashed
- 1 tbsp. of cumin seeds
- 1 tbsp. of turmeric
- 2 tbsp. of chili powder, red
- 1 handful of coriander leaves
- 1 tbsp. of dried herb gum (asafetida)
- Sugar, granulated, as needed
- 1 tbsp. of mango powder, dry, if available
- 2 cups of flour, wheat
- 4 tbsp. of oil, vegetable
- 2 tbsp. of powdered coriander
- 2 chopped chilies, green
- 2 tbsp. of lemon juice, fresh
- Sea salt, as needed
- 2 cups of water, filtered

Instructions:

1. Place a pan on med. heat. Pour some oil in and heat it. Add dried herb gum and cumin seeds. Stir till they begin to crackle.

2. Add mashed potatoes. Combine well. Add turmeric and chili powder, then coriander powder. Use sugar and salt as you need them. Stir thoroughly for three to four minutes.

3. Add filtered water as needed into pan. Stir for five more minutes. Add mango powder, green chilies and coriander leaves to pan. Stir for a short while. Turn heat off.

4. Transfer mixture (now called bhaji) to dish(es). Drizzle lemon juice over top.

5. For dough preparation, add oil and wheat flour to large bowl. Mix it well, using water as you need it. Knead and create soft dough.

6. Make small sized round balls from dough. Roll them and flatten to create puris.

7. Place a deep bottom pan and heat over med. heat. Pour some oil in and heat it. Once you've heated the oil, place one rolled puri in pan. Fry from both sides till the color is a golden brown.

8. Transfer puri to paper towels. Repeat with the rest of the puris. Serve fresh with bhaji.

11 – Amritsari Kulcha

This is one of the most authentic of North Indian meals. Stuffed kulchas are a crispy delight, served as Indian bread, made healthier since they are cooked in canola oil.

Makes 20 Servings

Cooking + Prep Time: 1 hour

Ingredients:

For dough

- 2 1/4 lbs. of flour, refined
- 13 1/2 fluid oz. of water, + extra if needed to make dough pliable

- 3 1/3 fluid oz. of oil, canola
- Optional: 1 pinch sea salt

For filling

- 1 cup of chopped onions
- 1 lb. of boiled, crushed potatoes
- 2 tsp. of roasted, crushed coriander seeds
- 2 tsp. of chopped ginger
- 2 to 3 chopped coriander sprigs
- 1 chopped chili, green
- 1 tbsp. of crushed pomegranate seed
- Lemon juice, fresh

Instructions:

1. Use the water, flour and salt to make semi-firm dough. Cover with moist kitchen towel for an hour in cool area.

2. Combine filling ingredients except for the oil. Fold gently together. Season as desired.

3. Dab oil on your palms and fingers. Using your hands, make balls about the size of medium potatoes with the dough. Flatten them. Pack with filling, enough to stuff and be encased.

4. Flatten the dough balls again using rolling pin.

5. Heat a nonstick pan on med. heat. Brush dough wedges with oil. Cook on both sides evenly. Serve with curd or chutney if you like.

12 – Punjabi-Style Okra

This is an easier variation on an older Indian dish with okra. Even kids eat okra when it's served in this dish! You can make it as spicy as you like, or as mild as you like. Serve it with yogurt or pitas for a speedy, tasty meal.

Makes 6 Servings

Cooking + Prep Time: 40 minutes

Ingredients:

- 1/3 cup of oil, vegetable
- 1/4 tsp. of mustard seed
- 1 pinch of powdered dry herb gum (asafetida)

- 1 sliced onion, medium
- 1 peeled, sliced garlic clove
- 1/4 tsp. of cumin seed
- 1/8 tsp. of turmeric, ground
- 1 chopped tomato, large
- 1 x 16-oz. pkg. of frozen okra, sliced
- 1/4 tsp. of chili powder
- 1 tsp. of sea salt, as desired

Instructions:

1. Heat the oil in skillet on med-high. Cook mustard seeds till they start crackling. Mix in the asafoetida. Reduce the heat down to low. Mix in turmeric, cumin seed, garlic and onion. Stir while cooking till onion becomes tender.

2. Stir okra and tomatoes into mixture. Mix in salt and chili powder gradually. Stir and cook for 8-10 minutes, till okra is firm but tender. Serve.

13 – Kadai Paneer with Tofu

This is a vegan version of paneer, made with tofu. It's nutritious, as well as delicious. The tofu cubes can be dunked in the creamy sauce, absorbing its flavor and spices. They make a great choice for potlucks or dinner parties.

Makes 6 Servings

Cooking + Prep Time: 35 minutes

Ingredients:

- 1 x 15-ounce block of cubed tofu, extra firm
- 3 diced tomatoes, large

- 1 tsp. of oil, vegetable
- 1 tsp. of cumin seeds
- 2 tbsp. of chopped cilantro leaves
- 1" of grated ginger, fresh
- 2 sliced shallots
- 1 tbsp. of coriander powder
- 1 heaping teaspoon of Garam masala spice blend
- 1/4 cup of cashews, raw

Instructions:

1. Heat oil in large sized sauce pan. Add cumin seeds. As they begin changing color, add tomatoes. Sauté tomatoes till they are thoroughly mashed and somewhat pulpy.

2. Add coriander leaves, ginger and shallots, then garam masala powder blend and coriander powder. Sauté for five more minutes. Add cubed tofu and 1 tbsp. of your prepared spice mix. Combine well.

3. Combine cashews with 1/2 cup of water to create cashew cream. Add to mixture and combine well. Add more salt if desired.

4. Allow the sauce to come to boil. Turn off heat. Serve hot.

14 – Kunna Mutton

This is a simple, scrumptious recipe that I'm betting your family will love. The Punjabi recipe has you cook the mutton with small-chopped veggies like turnips, tomatoes or radishes.

Makes 4 Servings

Cooking + Prep Time: 1 hour 40 minutes

Ingredients:

- 1 lb. of mutton
- 2 cups of tomatoes
- 2 tsp. of paste, garlic

- 2 tbsp. of yogurt (curd)
- 2 bay leaves
- 2 tsp. of red chili, dry
- 4 cloves
- 2 cardamom, green
- 1 turnip
- Salt, as desired
- 2 cups of onions
- 2 tsp. of paste, ginger
- 2 tsp. of powdered cumin
- 2 tbsp. of clarified butter
- 2 sticks of cinnamon
- 2 cardamom, black
- 2 radishes
- 5 carrots, baby

To garnish

- 1 tsp. of coriander leaves

Instructions:

1. Wash the pieces of mutton in running water. Pat them dry with a kitchen towel. Pour mutton pieces in large sized bowl.

Add salt to it, then add garlic paste, ginger and red chili powder. Allow it to marinate for a time.

2. Place earthen vessel over med. heat. Pour the clarified butter into it. Once butter has properly melted, add the whole spices. Add onions, too. Sauté till the onions are a golden brown. Add more garlic and ginger paste to vessel. Stir till its raw small is gone.

3. Add marinated pieces of mutton and dry spices. Once mutton has seared, add the chopped tomatoes. Let mutton cook awhile over low heat.

4. Once mutton is nearly cooked, add baby carrots, cut turnip and red radishes. Add whisked curd. Allow to sit on low heat for 10 more minutes.

5. Check the seasoning and adjust as desired. Garnish kunna meat with coriander leaves. Serve with naan flatbread or rice.

15 – Dhaba Dal

If you've wondered why the roadside vendors' food in ANY area is great, it's because the vendors make good use of local techniques and spices. This is abundantly true in North India. The recipes are handed down through the generations, and that's why the taste can't be beat.

Makes 3 Servings

Cooking + Prep Time: 45 minutes

Ingredients:

- 5 cups of water, filtered
- 1 cup of black gram (lentil), split

- 1/2 tsp. of turmeric, ground
- Salt, sea

To temper

- 1 tbsp. of butter, unsalted
- 1 tsp. of cumin seeds
- 1/2 tsp. of ginger, fresh
- 1 tsp. of garlic
- 2 slit chilies, green
- 1 minced onion, small
- 1 chopped tomato, small
- 1/4 cup of pureed tomatoes
- 2 tsp. of pre-made dhabba tadka lentil spice mix
- 1 fresh lemon, juice only

Instructions:

1. Cook dal with turmeric and salt.

2. Add 1 tbsp. butter to deep pan. Fry garlic and ginger.

3. Add onions. Cook till they are transparent.

4. Pour in cooked dal. Then add chopped tomatoes, salt and green chilies.

5. Wait a minute, then add dhaba tadka mix and tomato puree.

6. Top with lime juice and serve.

16 – Curry Pilaf

Here is a savory, delectable dish made with curried barley. It works wonderfully as a main dish, or you can serve it as a side with grilled chicken breast or fish. It's an impressive dish that is actually easy to make.

Makes 6 Servings

Cooking + Prep Time: 1 hour

Ingredients:

- 1/4 cup of butter, unsalted
- 1 diced onion, small
- 1 1/2 cups of barley, pearl

- 1/2 tsp. of allspice, ground
- 1/2 tsp. of turmeric, ground
- 1/4 tsp. of powdered curry
- 1/2 tsp. of salt, sea
- 1/8 tsp. of black pepper, ground
- 3 1/2 cups of broth, chicken
- 1/4 cup of almonds, slivered

Optional: 1/4 cup of raisins

Instructions:

1. Melt the butter in large sized skillet on med-high. Add barley and onions. Stir frequently while cooking till onion starts softening. Add and stir ground pepper, sea salt, curry powder, turmeric and allspice. Add broth. Bring to simmer.

2. Cover the skillet. Reduce the heat down to low. Simmer till barley becomes tender. Use a fork to fluff pilaf. Stir in raisins and almonds. Serve.

17 – Amritsari Fish

This dish is a wonderful treat for people who love fish. The fish pieces are coated with a spicy batter, before being deep-fried. As a garnish, garam masala spice blend and a bit of fresh lemon juice give it a special zing.

Makes 2 Servings

Cooking + Prep Time: 25 minutes + 3 hours setting time

Ingredients:

- 2 1/4 lbs. of fish
- Salt, sea, as desired

For batter

- 1 cup of flour, gram
- 2 tsp. of Garam masala spice mix
- 1 tsp. of chili powder, red
- 2 tsp. of powdered cumin
- Salt, sea, as desired
- 1 tsp. of powdered turmeric
- Filtered water, as needed
- Lemon juice, fresh, as desired

To deep fry: oil

Instructions:

1. To prepare batter, add turmeric, sea salt, chili powder, cumin powder, Garam masala, flour and sufficient water to give a coating consistency to batter in large bowl. Combine well.

2. Clean fish. Slice into pieces. Add sea salt. Set aside for three hours.

3. Wash salt off. Coat fish pieces with batter.

4. Deep fry till fish is finished cooking. Garnish using lemon juice and Garam masala. Serve while hot.

18 – Dal Makhani

Dal Makhani is a staple in the Punjab region of India. It is now served in other areas of India, too, and in some foreign countries. You can easily cook it at home. It's great for dinner – or a dinner party.

Makes 4 Servings

Cooking + Prep Time: 55 minutes

Ingredients:

- 2 cups of dal, Sabut urad
- 8 cups of water, filtered
- 2 tbsp. of salt, sea
- 1 tbsp. of sliced ginger
- 2 tbsp. of butter, unsalted
- 1 tbsp. of oil, olive
- 2 tsp. of black cumin (Shahi jeera)
- 1 tsp. of fenugreek (Kasoori meethi)
- 2 cups of tomato puree
- 1 tsp. of sugar, granulated
- 1 tsp. of chili powder
- 1/2 cup of cream

To garnish: lengthways-slit chilies, green

Instructions:

1. Add ginger, water and 1 tbsp. sea salt to dal. Cook till dal is tender.

2. Heat oil and butter in heavy pan. Add fenugreek and black cumin. When they are spluttering, add the sugar, chili powder, remaining sea salt and tomato puree.

3. Stir-fry on high heat till oil has separated.

4. Add the cooked dal. Bring to boil. Consistency should allow dal to move freely around when you stir it. If it isn't, add a bit more water and stir.

5. Allow to sit uncovered to simmer until blended well. Add cream. Once it heats through, garnish with green chilies and serve promptly.

19 – Tandoori Chicken

Cooks in the Punjab region are some of the keepers of the style of cooking known as tandoori. These dishes are easily recreated in your own home, and the taste is fantastic.

Makes 4 Servings

Cooking + Prep Time: 1 1/4 hour

Ingredients:

- 8 skin-on chicken pieces - breasts, thighs, wings
- Oil, as needed

For marinade

- 4 tsp. of chili paste, red
- 3 tbsp. of garlic and ginger paste
- 2 tsp. of Chaat masala spice powder
- 1 tbsp. of oil, olive
- 1 1/2 tsp. of Tandoori Masala
- 3 tbsp. of curd
- Se salt, as desired
- 1/2 fresh lemon, juice only

For tandoori masala

- 2 cinnamon sticks
- 1 tbsp. of peppercorns, black
- Cardamom pods, 3 brown and 5 green
- 2 tsp. of cumin seeds
- 2 tsp. of coriander seeds
- 1 bay leaf
- 3 cloves
- 3/4 tsp. of turmeric

Instructions:

1. For tandoori masala, dry roast turmeric powder, bay leaf, cloves, cumin seeds, coriander seeds, all cardamom, peppercorns and cinnamon.

2. Grind roasted spices into a powder in mortar and pestle.

3. Add garlic and ginger paste to medium bowl, along with lemon juice, sea salt, curd, oil, tandoori masala, chaat masala and red chili paste. Combine well.

4. Rub marinade on chicken, both over and under skin. Make small sized incisions in chicken for marinade.

5. Marinate chicken for 1/2 hour.

6. Char-grill chicken on grill. Baste with oil while grilling. Serve with wedges of fresh lemon.

20 – Mutton Curry

Mutton curry is one of the most popular meals among foodies in India, who love delicious, spicy dishes. It uses many wholesome spices cooked in clarified butter. It's quite the mouth-watering delight.

Makes 6 Servings

Cooking + Prep Time: 45 minutes

Ingredients:

- 17 1/2 oz. of mutton
- 4 onions, sliced
- 2 tbsp. of powdered coriander
- 4 cloves
- 2 tsp. of garlic, crushed into paste
- 5 cardamom, green
- 1 stick of cinnamon
- Salt, as needed
- 2 cups of water, filtered
- 4 tbsp. of clarified butter
- 2 cups of yogurt, curd
- 2 tsp. of ginger, crushed into paste
- 2 tsp. of chili powder, red
- 3 tomatoes, mashed
- 8 peppercorns
- 1 tsp. of powdered Garam masala
- 1/2 tsp. of turmeric powder

To garnish

- 1 handful of coriander leaves, chopped

Instructions:

1. Wash and clean mutton. Heat clarified butter in frying pan.

2. Add stick of cinnamon, peppercorns, cloves and cardamom. Sauté for one minute. Add onions and salt. Sauté till onion becomes light brown.

3. Add garlic and ginger paste. Cook mixture till its raw smell has disappeared.

4. Add coriander powder, turmeric powder and red chili powder to mixture. Combine well. Add mashed tomatoes. Mix well. Be sure tomatoes become pulpy. Cook mixture till oil has separated from masala.

5. Add mutton to masala. Mix well. Make sure pieces of mutton are coated evenly with the masala.

6. Add yogurt to masala mutton. Mix well. Allow to cook for four or five minutes. Add water. Stir well. Check seasoning. Add coriander leaves and garam masala. Stir quickly.

7. Cook for 20-30 minutes, ensuring that the mutton is fully cooked and nicely juicy. After it is done, remove from heat. Transfer to bowl. Serve hot with naan flatbread or rice.

21 – Punjabi Saag

Saag is an Indian curry with cooked bitter greens, like mustard, turnip, spinach, collard greens or kale. You can also use beet greens, Bok choy or chard. Any green combination will work. Add more peppers and spices if you want a hotter saag.

Makes 6 Servings

Cooking + Prep Time: 55 minutes

Ingredients:

- 1/2 cup of butter, unsalted

- 2 tsp. of cumin seed
- 1 seeded, diced chili pepper, green
- 2 chopped garlic cloves
- 2 tbsp. of turmeric, ground
- 1 lb. of chopped spinach, fresh
- 1 lb. of chopped mustard greens, fresh
- 1 tsp. of ground coriander
- 1 tsp. of ground cumin
- 1 tsp. of salt, sea

Instructions:

1. In large sized skillet, melt butter on med-high. While cooking, add and stir turmeric, garlic, chili pepper and cumin seed till fragrant.

2. Add spinach and mustard greens and stir. Add thicker leaves and stems first. Continue adding greens. Cook while stirring till you have added all greens and they are all wilted thoroughly.

3. Stir in sea salt, cumin and coriander. Cover skillet. Lower heat. Simmer till greens become tender. Add water sufficient to keep greens moist. Serve hot.

22 – Spiced Lentils

Far from the hot-spicy types of Indian recipes, Dal Tadka offers lentils with comforting, warm spices. It's most appreciated when the weather is colder. It's a creamy, feel-good meal with the tanginess of tomatoes and the warmth of spices and garlic.

Makes 6 Servings

Cooking + Prep Time: 45 minutes

Ingredients:

- 1/2 cup of pigeon peas, split
- 1/2 cup of lentils, pink

- 1/2 cup of lentils, mung
- 1/2 tsp. of turmeric, ground
- 1 tsp. of oil, coconut
- 1 tsp. of mustard seeds
- 2 dry chilies, red
- 4 minced garlic cloves
- 1 diced tomato, large
- 1 tsp. of sugar, granulated
- Salt, sea, as desired
- 2 tbsp. of lemon juice, fresh
- 2 tbsp. of minced coriander leaves

Instructions:

1. Wash, combine and cook lentils with turmeric. Cover in pan with 1-inch water.

2. Bring the lentils to boil. Cover pan. Set on low heat. Allow lentils to simmer for 35-40 minutes, till lentils are very soft and easy to mash. Add water as needed while you're cooking the lentils.

3. Heat oil in sauce pan. Add red chilies and mustard seeds. When seeds are sputtering and crackling, add garlic. Stir-fry till garlic has browned. Stir constantly and don't allow garlic to burn.

4. Add tomato. Cook for several minutes, till tomato has broken down.

5. Add water and lentils. Bring to boil. Allow to cook for several minutes.

6. Add salt and sugar. Stir and combine. Add coriander and mix well. Turn heat off. Serve while hot with parathas or rice.

23 – Ginger Mustard Meat Roti

This is a classic dish in the Punjab region, especially popular during the winter months. It includes green, ginger-infused mustard with white butter, honey or jaggery. Along with hot bread, it Makes a wonderful treat.

Makes 4 Servings

Cooking + Prep Time: 2 1/2 hours

Ingredients:

For the saag

- 1 1/2 lb. of mustard green and spice mixture - Sarson Saag
- 8 3/4 oz. of spinach greens - Palak Saag
- 8 3/4 oz. of green leafy vegetable mixture - Bathua Saag
- 1 cup of water, filtered
- 1 pinch salt, sea
- 1 1/2 cup of corn meal - Makki atta
- 4 chilies, green
- 3/4 oz. of ginger, fresh
- 2 onions, small
- 6 garlic cloves
- 3 1/2 oz. of clarified butter
- 1/2 tsp. of pepper powder, red
- 1/2 tsp. of Garam masala spice blend
- 1/2 tsp. of powdered coriander

For the Makki ki Roti

- 1 lb. of corn meal - Makki Atta
- Water, to knead

- Clarified butter, to fry

Instructions:

1. Add three saags plus water and sea salt into a pressure cooker. Cook on low for 1 1/2 hours.

2. Squeeze saag out and keep the saag water to the side. Mash the saag in cooker till ground coarsely. Add corn meal. Stir well.

3. Put the saag water back. Add some fresh water. Boil on low heat.

4. Add ginger and green chilies. Cook until saag becomes thicker.

5. Add garam masala, red pepper powder, garlic, ginger and chopped onions. Sauté till the onions become light brown. Mix it into saag. Garnish with julienne sliced ginger fried in the clarified butter.

6. Knead corn meal till it has become a ball. Add the atta. Knead.

7. Heat tava. Add a bit of clarified butter so it won't stick.

8. Create round shapes from makki roti. Transfer to tava.

9. Cook with clarified butter till they are golden brown. Serve with butter.

24 – Punjabi Chick Peas

This is one of the best slow cooker Punjabi recipes you will find. All you have to do is pour the ingredients into your slow cooker and a few hours later, you can lay a fragrant, delicious meal in front of your family.

Makes 8 Servings

Cooking + Prep Time: 20 minutes + 6 hours slow cooker time

Ingredients:

- 1 x 29-ounce can of drained chick peas
- 1 onion, medium
- 2 tomatoes, large
- 2 tbsp. of tomato paste
- 4 garlic cloves
- 1" chopped ginger piece
- 2 bay leaves
- 1/2 tsp. of powdered cumin seeds
- 1 tbsp. of powdered coriander seeds
- 1 tbsp. of powdered chana masala or Garam masala spice mix
- 1/4 tsp. of turmeric, ground
- 1 tsp. of chaat masala
- 1 tsp. of paprika
- 1 tsp. of cayenne, +/- as desired

To garnish: 1/4 cup of coriander, chopped

- Sea salt, as desired

Instructions:

1. Puree ginger, garlic, tomatoes and onions.

2. Place in slow cooker with remainder of ingredients, except for coriander leaves and salt.

3. Add 3 cups of filtered water. Set slow cooker on the high setting.

4. Allow chana masala to cook for about six hours. Add water now and then as needed.

5. After six hours have elapsed, add coriander leaves and salt. Combine thoroughly. Serve with roti's or rice.

25 – Punjabi Butter Chicken

Butter chicken has been a hit among residents of India and visitors, too, particularly if they want a real taste of authentic Indian cooking. There are multiple versions of the original of this recipe, but however it started, it's delicious, and it's a hit.

Makes 8 Servings

Cooking + Prep Time: 1 hour

Ingredients:

- 1 1/2 lbs. of chicken, raw

For marinade

- 1 tsp. of chili powder, red
- 1 tsp. of garlic and ginger paste
- Salt, sea, as desired
- 8 oz. of curd

For gravy

- 6 oz. of butter, unsalted
- 1/2 tsp. of cumin seeds, black
- 17 1/2 oz. of pureed tomatoes
- 1/2 tsp. of sugar, granulated
- 1 tsp. of chili powder, red
- Salt, sea, as desired
- 3 1/2 oz. of cream, fresh
- 4 sliced chilies, green
- 1/2 tsp. of crushed fenugreek leaves

Instructions:

1. For marinade, mix curd, salt, garlic ginger paste and red chili powder in medium sized bowl.

2. Add pieces of raw chicken to marinade. Combine fully. Keep in fridge overnight.

3. Roast marinated chicken in oven for 9-12 minutes, till it's 3/4 done.

4. Heat 1/2 of butter in pan.

5. Add pureed tomatoes. Sauté for a few minutes. Add sea salt, red chili powder, sugar and cumin seeds. Combine well.

6. Add prepared chicken, along with fenugreek leaves, sliced chilies, fresh cream and butter. Sauté for three to four minutes. Allow chicken to cook.

7. Cook until the chicken is completed cooked. Serve with flatbread or rice.

Delectable Punjabi Dessert Recipes...

26 – Malai Peda

These sweets are so soft you'll swear they are melting in your mouth. They are a hit at any gathering. They take less than a half-hour to prepare, so they're a quick treat to make.

Makes 10 Servings

Cooking + Prep Time: 20 minutes

Ingredients:

- 1 tin of milk, sweetened, condensed
- 1 tbsp. of clarified butter, pure
- 3 tbsp. of whitener, dairy
- 1/2 cup of milk, whole
- 1 tsp. of flour, corn

- 2 tbsp. of lime juice, fresh

Instructions:

1. Mix all ingredients together.

2. Heat in heavy pan. Stir constantly while cooking until the mixture thickens and starts leaving pan sides.

3. Remove from heat. Allow to cool and shape the dough into pedas dessert pieces. Serve.

27 – Rice Kheer

Kheer is made from rice and milk, and it's very basic and simple, but very sweet, too. It has long been used in religious celebrations in India, in almost all the religions practiced there. It was once offered to deities during Indian religious ceremonies.

Makes 10 Servings

Cooking + Prep Time: 25 minutes

Ingredients:

- 33 3/4 fluid oz. of milk, full fat
- 3 1/2 oz. of rice, basmati
- 2 3/4 oz. of sugar, granulated
- 32 fluid oz. of water, filtered
- 32 fluid oz. of milk, evaporated
- 1 tbsp. of almonds, chopped
- 1 tbsp. of raisins, golden

Instructions:

1. Wash rice. You don't have to soak it or it could make mushy kheer.

2. Place pan on med. heat. Add milk. Bring to boil.

3. Add rice. Stir over med-low heat. Don't allow rice to stick to pan bottom.

4. After several minutes, rice will be cooked and floating to milk surface.

5. Continue to stir as the mixture becomes creamy.

6. Add raisins and chopped almonds. Add sugar. Stir well.

7. Add some of the evaporated milk to thicken the kheer up and give it a creamy color and texture.

8. Turn heat off. Keep pan covered. Serve for dessert.

28 – Kaju Katli

This dish has popularity over the entire subcontinent of India. It has a spongy and smooth texture, with long lasting taste. There are only a few steps needed to make this treat, and your family or guests will love it.

Makes 5 Servings

Cooking + Prep Time: 40 minutes

Ingredients:

- 7 fluid oz. of milk, sweetened and condensed
- 5 1/3 oz. of cashews

- 5 1/3 oz. of dried milk solids (khoa)
- 1 3/4 oz. of flour, wheat - Maida
- 1/2 cup of milk, whole

Instructions:

1. Crush the cashews till you have a very fine powder.

2. Place all ingredients together. Grind and mix into smooth-textured paste.

3. Transfer mixture to heavy-bottomed pan. Cook on low till mixture begins to leave pan sides, forming a ball.

4. Place mixture on tray. Roll out to 1/8-inch thickness. Cool. Cut them into pieces the shape of diamonds. Serve.

29 – Saffron and Sweet Rice

Meethe rice has been, and still is, served at auspicious occasions in India. Saffron is usually added to the sweet for greater flavor and color.

Makes various servings depending on size

Cooking + Prep Time: 50 minutes

Ingredients:

- 1/2 cup of rice, basmati
- 2 tbsp. of oil, cooking

- 1 stick of cinnamon

- 2 bay leaves

- 2 cardamom pods, black

- 4 cardamom pods, green

- 1 cup of sugar, granulated

- 1 tbsp. of raisins

- 1 tbsp. of almonds, slivered

- 1 tbsp. of milk, warm

- 2 cups of water, filtered

- 1 tsp. of turmeric, for yellow color

Instructions:

1. Wash rice. Allow it to soak for 10-15 minutes or so.

2. Cook rice in filtered water. Add the turmeric as you cook, to give the rice that yellow color you want.

3. Add cooking oil to non-stick pan over med. heat.

4. Add cinnamon stick, all cardamom pods, cloves and bay leaves.

5. Add in cooked rice. Combine well by stirring. Add sugar. Combine again.

6. Add milk with dissolved Saffron to rice. Combine thoroughly. Garnish as desired. Serve.

30 – Kalakand

This is a quick recipe for kalakand, which takes much less time than the traditional recipe did. It's so easy to make right in your kitchen. They key to great taste is making sure you include all the right ingredients in their proper proportions.

Makes 25 pieces

Cooking + Prep Time: 3 1/2 hours

Ingredients:

- 2 1/4 cups of cottage cheese, grated
- 1 1/2 cups of powdered milk

- 1 1/2 cups of cream, fresh
- 3/4 cup of sugar, granulated
- 1/2 tsp. of cardamom powder

For garnishing

- 1 tbsp. of slivered almonds
- 1 tbsp. of slivered pistachio nuts

Instructions:

1. Mix all ingredients except powdered cardamom in non-stick pan. Combine well.

2. Cook over med. heat for 12-15 minutes. Mixture should have thickened and left sides of pan, towards the center. Stir constantly as it cooks. Scrape down pan sides.

3. Remove from heat. Add powdered cardamom. Combine thoroughly.

4. Transfer mixture to 7-inch platter. Spread evenly.

5. Garnish using slivered pistachios and almonds. Pat lightly so they'll stick. Set aside and allow to cool for three hours.

6. Cut in pieces to serve.

Conclusion

This Punjabi cookbook has shown you…

…How to use different ingredients to affect unique Indian tastes in dishes both well-known and rare. It is becoming a more popular way of cooking worldwide.

How can you include North Indian cuisine in your home recipes?

You can…

- Make Punjabi breakfast dishes, which vary in different Punjab regions. You may enjoy the flatbread paratha or poori, served with the sweet dish halwa.
- Learn to cook dal, which is commonly found in Punjabi meals. It's prepared with tasty lentils and seasoned with aromatic and spice mixtures, which enhance the taste.
- Enjoy making the delectable vegetarian dishes of the Punjab region, made with many wonderful ingredients like potatoes, cauliflower, onion, eggplants, tomatoes and

curry spices. There are SO many ways to make them great.

- Make meat and seafood dishes, which often use goat, lamb, fish and eggs. Using beef for meat-based meals is not allowed in India's Punjab region. The variety of fish include catfish, tilapia and carp.
- Make various types of Punjabi desserts and cakes that will tempt your family's sweet tooth.

Have fun experimenting! Enjoy the results!

Made in the USA
Monee, IL
07 April 2021